HOW TO
CATCH
ᵃLIAR

••NOTE••

How to Catch a Liar contains many of the very same

techniques and procedures used, and indicators

of lying sought, by police detectives.

Please use responsibly.

STEVEN DAVID LAMPLEY

WHAT PEOPLE ARE SAYING

"THE THING I LIKE ABOUT STEVEN, HE HAS ALL THIS FORENSIC KNOWLEDGE AND HE CAN TAKE ALL THAT INFORMATION AND RELAY IT IN A WAY THAT EVERYBODY CAN UNDERSTAND."
Nancy Grace
Grace & Abrams
A&E Network
Crime Stories with Nancy Grace

"HIS SKILLS PLACE HIM IN THE 'CREAM OF THE CROP' CATEGORY."
William T. Gaut, PhD.
(Former Deputy Chief, Homicide Division)

"POLICE OFFICER TO POLICE OFFICER, YOU'RE AT LEGEND STATUS!"
Ryan Patterson
(Law Enforcement)

"MEET A MOST INCREDIBLE MAN. HE'S LIKE SHERLOCK HOLMES AND 'LIE TO ME' ALL IN ONE: DETECTIVE AND AUTHOR"
Anne Terri
(Writer/Director)

HOW TO
CATCH
a LIAR

OTHER BOOKS
By
Steven David Lampley

How to Have the Psychological Advantage

Outside Your Door

The Dahmer Book

Inside the Mind of a Serial Killer

True Crime Facts You May Not Know

Printed in the United States of America

Oliphant Publishing

Third Edition. First Printing, 2017

ISBN-13: 9781793964809

DEDICATION

I want to dedicate this to my mom and dad.

      My dad was killed when I was just nine years old, a catastrophic event in my life, one that I am not ashamed to say impacts me until this very day. Before he died, however, he was the owner of his own business, Lampley Tool and Die in Gallatin, Tennessee (just outside Nashville, Tennessee). He owned the business and never had to go into work on the weekends, yet he did. He did, because his clients were very important to him. He worked tirelessly to make sure each client was totally satisfied and happy with his company and the product he supplied them. My dad is where I learned my work ethic and how to treat people. Truth is, my dad died after falling asleep one early morning a 3:00 a.m. on his way back home from a business trip to meet with one of his clients. After he fell asleep, his foot hit the accelerator and climbed to a speed estimated by police to be in excess of 120 miles per hour. His car left the roadway and hit a concrete culvert sending his car airborne and, for a distance of 300 feet his car flipped and flipped until it came to a rest upside down in the middle of the highway. Ironically, this accident occurred right in front of my mom's and dad's best friends home. It was Lewis, my mom's and dad's best friend, who heard the wreck and found my dad.

My mom raised my brother and I the best she could. We moved out of the house my dad had custom-built for my mom and we moved closer to Nashville. Funny, sometimes the things you remember, but I remember my mom always wanted an octagon-shaped window in the bathroom and my dad had her a custom window made for the bathroom! My mom worked her ass off to care for us. Mom taught me to respect everyone, regardless of any education, social standing, race, belief, or creed. She was a small woman, but with a Tasmanian attitude if you messed with her "boys." Mom was always there to kiss the hurts, to listen, to help any way she could. From her, I also learned compassion.

My parents were good people – good parents.

Miss you mom and dad.

Steven David Lampley

"I'm not upset that you lied to me, I'm upset that from now on I can't believe you"

Friedrich Nietzsche

HOW TO
CATCH a LIAR

INTRODUCTION

People lie and, well, there's not a who lot we can do to stop their lying. However, we can improve our skills in detecting these lies and catching the liars in their tracks!

I have found since I wrote the first edition of this book that it had a couple of unexpected consequences.

Firstly, I had a couple of individuals purchase the book and simply had it lying around. Before they even had a chance to read it, it garnered the attention of their teenage children who changed their behavior.

Secondly, it seems that there are times when someone will read this book (or attend one of my How to Catch a Liar Training Sessions) and others find out, then some of those people seem to become distant from the HTCAL reader!

As the author, I also find the same thing. People will change their behavior around me or, when introduced to someone new and they find out I am the author of HTCAL, they find an excuse to leave the convo. Either way, it is a very revealing response.

Being able to discern lies is an amazing skill set applicable to business as well as one's personal life.

Whether contract negotiations, employment interviews, parent and child convos, or even in a dating situation, being able to pick out lies has an obvious advantage.

Read this book, become a student of the craft. Watch people. Go online and watch videos of people who were interviewed and who were later revealed as lying during that interview. Watch for the indicators, they're there!

Lastly, I would love to come to your corporation, business, college or university, organization, or work with you to organized a for-the-public event! The live seminar has multiple videos and, not only is there a lot of information, we have fun with it as well!

Enjoy your book and thank you for purchasing a copy!

Steven David Lampley

CHAPTER ONE

Background

I was at a book signing back some time ago with the first edition of this book and was sitting at my black cloth draped table and my How to Catch a Liar books prominently displayed. An older couple walked in the bookstore and proceeded into the store. In a little while, the husband came to my table and introduced himself. A nice, pleasant, well-spoken man, we were having a good conversation when his wife also walked up beside him. His wife was one of those bubbly, butterfly personalities, always happy and smiling. She had her purchases in her bag, looked at him and said, "Hey baby, watcha doin?"

"I'm talking with Mr. Lampley about his book. I think I'm going to buy a copy."

She looked at his hand, as he had previously picked up a copy, and, instead of looking at the table, asked, "What book is that, honey?"

He turned the book around so she could see the front cover and I watched her face. It was like someone pulled a shade down on her face! That bubbly smile vanished and she, in a mater of fact voice, "Oh, honey, you don't need that book!"

[Ever get in one of those situations where you just want to disappear or crawl under a rock? I was here!]

"Oh, I know, but I think it'd be neat to learn how to catch liars."

Again, as if a second shade was pulled down over her face, a look, almost of contempt, displayed across her face. "I SAID, YOU DON'T NEED THAT BOOK!!" and stormed out of the store, alone. I watched the man's face and it was if nothing had happened! He looked up at me, held his hand out to shake my hand and, after our handshake, he took the book to the cashier, paid for it, and left the store.

After the gentleman left the store, I

thought to myself how very appreciative I was that I was not the officer who was going to be working the beat in their neighborhood that night!

. . .

One of the questions I get frequently is, how prevalent is lying? I'm not sure that prevalent is the correct word, the word rampant seems to fit the question better!

How rampant is lying? Well, just in the business world, lying and deception accounts for around one trillion dollars in losses each year. Yes! One trillion, that's a one with nine zeros! Looks like this: $1,000,000,000!!

Of course, the lies that contributed to that astronomical figure are moreover the worst of the lies told and include the lies and deception that include embezzlement, theft, and similar.

Thankfully, most lies account for small, white lies that, normally, don't have a negative impact on anyone. You've heard them, you've probably even told them before.

"Oh, honey, that dress looks marvelous on you!" [When it really makes her look like an Andy Warhol painted circus tent.]

"If you don't behave, Santa won't leave you any presents!" [No, I'm not saying to ditch Santa!]

"Oh baby, the lasagna you cooked was awesome!" [When it shriveled up to the size of a hockey puck and was just as hard!]

"I'm so, so sick [cough, cough] I won't be able to come to work today." [No explanation needed...lol]

"I didn't get your text message."

"I don't care what restaurant we go to."

"No, I don't want that last hot, gooey, delicious, brownie."

The list goes on.

Women, statistically, will tell around three to four lies each day while men, statistically, will tell around five or six lies each day.

Women, for the most part, tell lies of tact and comfort. Lies like "Oh, baby it will be okay" when they really know it will not be okay. "Girlfriend, that dress is the bomb!" when you really mean it looked like a bomb exploded on it!

Men, moreover, will tell lies that make them look better. Lies of ego and self-aggrandizement. Lies such as, "When I was just a mere child of ten, I wrestled a bear to the ground!" [Yeah, okay, whatever.] "I am a top secret spy for the government." [Single ladies, ever heard that one?]

Beside the little white lies, there are lies told to try to keep people out of trouble.

"No, I didn't eat the last piece of cake."

"I didn't know that was yours."

And in my former line of work, "Officer, I only had two beers." [Two 55 gallon drums!]

Then we go to the big league lies, lies that are criminal in nature.

"No, I didn't rob that bank."

"I never hit him!"

"I don' know who killed him, but it wasn't me!"

"The money in the escrow account was still there last time I checked."

With all that being said, how good are we at detecting lies? Studies show that someone who has not received proper training in lie detection can only detect lies approximately 54 percent of the time. Not very good! Heck, without training, one might as well just not worry about trying to figure out if a statement is a lie, make it easy, and just flip a coin! The accuracy will be just about as good and it saves a lot of worry and headache trying to figure out if it was a lie or not! Studies also show that someone who *has* received proper training in detecting lies can do so about 90 percent of the time! A **huge** difference!

Let me end this introduction with a few interesting tidbits regarding lies and lying.

• More lies are old in January than any other month.

• When you meet someone new, you will

typically hear two to three lies in the first ten minutes of the conversation.

- You are typically lied to more in writing than face-to-face.
- People tend to believe men with beards more so than men who do not have beards.
- The more we lie, the easier it is for us to justify it to ourselves. It's a brain thing.
- Studies show it is generally harder for people to lie to those they think are attractive.
- Lying is not exclusive to humans! Nope! In fact, both plants and animals can be deceptive. Take, for instance, the Venus Fly Trap, a carnivorous plant that produces a sweet nectar for the purpose of luring insects into their trap to be eaten for their next meal! Chameleons can change color to blend into their environment. Perhaps the best example of an animal lying is the gorilla, Hanabiko, known the world-over as Koko. Koko is no longer with us (she passed away in 2018), but when she was living, her fame came from the fact that she could communicate with humans! She did so,

by way of her relatively large vocabulary of American Sign Language (ASL) of approximately 1,000 signs and could comprehend about 2,000 words. On one occasion, Koko broke her sink. When she was asked how the sink became broken, she signed that "the cat did it."

CHAPTER TWO
Misconceptions

I find in my travels and seminars that there are a few predominant beliefs among a large number of people who think that certain mannerisms are immediately indicative of a liar. Unfortunately, that is not true.

MISCONCEPTION ONE

"If they don't look me in my eyes when they talk to me, then they are lying to me."

Nope!

His is probably THE most erroneous belief about lying I come across.

Yes, before we get started, someone not looking another in their eyes when talking is an indicator or lying, but a very poor indicator.

[We will discuss this a lot more in depth in a coming chapter, but let me say it now: "Any indicator used alone or without establishing a baseline can be errant and provide inaccurate information.]

There can be several reasons why someone may not look you in your eyes when they are talking to you.

1. Someone who has Asperger's may be uncomfortable looking you in your eyes when they talk to you.

2. Someone with PTSD (Post-Traumatic Stress Disorder) may not be comfortable looking you in your eyes when they talk to you.

3. Someone who has a low self-esteem may not be comfortable looking you in your eyes when they talk to you.

4. Someone who is shy may not be comfortable looking you in your eyes when they talk to you.

5. Someone who has been the vicim of physical or verbal abuse my not be comfortable looking you in your eyes when they talk to you.

So, by using this indicator, especially as a stand-alone and/or without establishing a baseline, can yield you totally erroneous information regarding whether or not that person is lying. By using this one indicator, you will label those people in those five situations as liars when, in fact, they may very well be telling you the truth! What a travesty to them and to you! Don't do it!

But it gets worse!

There are those who I call professional liars, they lie all the time about most anything and everything. Typically psychopathic, they are attuned to the fact that most people believe the *if they won't look me in my eyes they're lying* mantra and will, on purpose, stare in your eyes to keep from looking away!

So, you use this one indicator and, not only are you labeling potentially innocent people as liars, you are also believing the professional liar because they look at you with purposeful determination!

MISCONCEPTION TWO

"If someone is talking to me with their arms crossed, they are lying to me."

Nope!

This is another really common belief that is errant.

Just because someone has their arms crossed does not automatically signify lies are ensuing! Folks, we don't go around town with our arms dangling at our sides 24/7 like zombies! Sometimes, it's just simply more comfortable to cross our arms! It's physiology! When our arms are outstretched, certain muscles are relaxed and some are contracted – some muscles are working and some are resting! When we cross our arms the muscles switch and the muscles that were contracted are now resting! But wait, there's more!

Have you ever been chilled? No, I'm not talking about being in the arctic north, I'm simply taking about being chilled slightly or cold, maybe even in an air conditioned room where it may be comfortable for others, but cool to you? I bet you crossed your arms a some point. If you were talking to someone and they had the misbelief that if someone crosses their arms hey are lying, then guess what? They probably thought you were lying to them!

Again, sometimes it's just more comfortable to cross our arms!

If you are using either of these as your go-to for determining if someone is lying to you, ahem...STOP!

CHAPTER THREE
Housekeeping

You can learn all of the indicators of lying, but unless you know how to apply them, the indicators are pretty much unreliable. Let's discuss some of these.

CLUSTERING

Individual indicators of lying can, and do, reveal lies, but it is preferred that we see two, maybe three, indicators in one short sequence. The more indicators, the more likely we have a lie.

These clusters may consist of either verbal or physical indicators, or a combination of the two. For instance, you have asked someone a question and the other person rubs his neck and then adjusts his necktie. Both of those actions are physical indicators of a lie. Maybe, instead, the person's vocal tone became higher and she began stuttering. Both of those are verbal indicators of a lie. However, you may also find that the other person may exhibit both physical and verbal indicators. That person may rub his neck and stutter when he answers.

TIMING OF INDICATORS

Indicators of lying may occur at any time in a conversation, but we particularly are interested in the indicators shown in the first six seconds of the subject's answer after we ask a question or make a statement to them.

SYNERGISTIC

Observation. You **must** be observant and observe the subject's entire body. We are not just looking for some rote, on-the-list indicators, we have to observe the entire body, head to toe and put what we see together in a package.

This is a total body, simultaneous process. Simultaneous, Steven? Yep! You may observe the display of more than one indicator at the same time.

The liar could possibly exhibit two or

more physical indicators while talking and, while the physical indicators are being displayed, provide verbal indicators as well!

Open your eyes and prep your ears! Lie detecting is a very active process and one that is dependent on keen observation!

BASELINE

There are some advocates who say a baseline is not necessary. While it may not be necessary, it is a tremendous help! Regardless of the argument, it helps to know the mannerisms of an individual, how they act, how they talk, and how they react to certain stimuli.

I usually will ask someone some questions I know they will more than likely answer truthfully, like "What is your name again, I'm sorry, I forgot?" "What did you have for dinner?" "I love your shoes, where did you get them?"

I will watch their body position; arm, hand, leg, feet, and head movements; and I will listen to their words and vocal tonation.

No, a baseline is not absolutely necessary, but I had rather have one than not.

ALCOHOL OR DRUGS

If you are trying to determine if someone is lying to you, it is best to avoid doing so if (s)he is under the influence of drugs and/or alcohol. Not only can it mar the otherwise obvious lying indicators the alcohol and/or drugs can impair their thoughts, memory, and reasoning.

IMPORTANT CONCEPTS SELF-CHECK

1. Clustering of lying indicators only pertains to verbal indicators.   T   F

2. We are very interested in the indicators of lying in the first _____ seconds of the beginning of someone's answer or statement. 6, 10, 12, 15

3. A cluster of indicators means that we need a minimum of twelve indicators for the statement to be a lie.   T   F

4. A baseline is where we are talking to two individuals at the same time about an incident and we begin talking to them at the same time, the baseline.   T   F

5. Clustering, timing, synergy, and the baseline are not necessary to properly discern whether or not someone is lying to us.   T   F

Answers on next page. Oh, come on, you didn't think I was going to put the answers on the same page as the questions did you?

ANSWERS

1. F
2. 6
3. F
4. F
5. F

CHAPTER FOUR
Fight or Flight

Fight-or-flight is a physiological response of the body to a perceived threat. When a threat is observed, the body activates a series of events inside the body in response to that threat.

Due to the activation of several parts of the body, the flight-or-fight response can cause a variety of signs which can include:

- Shaking
- Dilation of pupils
- Dilation of blood vessels in muscles to supply more blood to the muscles in preparation of fighting or fleeing
- Constriction of blood vessels in parts of the body
- Tachycardia (increased heartbeat)
- Tachypnea (increased breathing)
- Involuntary urination (Ooooops!)
- Pale skin

- Tunnel vision

- Digestion slows

- Decreased salivation and tears

- Loss of, or decreased, hearing

- Blood pressure increase to help supply energy to the body for fighting or fleeing

- Muscle tension that can provide the body with additional strength to fight or flee and the energy to make that happen

When stressed, the liar may exhibit these signs.

CHAPTER FIVE
Verbal Indicators

Verbal indicators consist of a plethora of things that include words used and words not used, vocal tone, inflections, pronoun usage, contraction usage, language formality, the manner in which words are said, and even the absence of speech!

INDICATORS

Singing the word, "No"

If someone answers you and they answer using the word "No" as if they are singing the word, that is an indicator that they are lying. That can be vocal inflection that begins in a lower tone and carries out into a higher tone. "nooooooooo" is an example. They may also sing the word "no" starting in a higher pitch and going lower then back up again or begin lower, go high, and then back low.

Elimination of Contractions

Someone who is lying will typically use more formal language and, as such, will eliminate contractions.

For instance, if you suspect Bill stole some money and you ask him, "Did you take the money from the counter?" and his reply is "No, I did not take that money." That may indicate a lie. Had he said, "No, I didn't take that money," he may be telling the truth.

Pronoun Usage

Often, people involved in a bad situation or crime will try to distance themselves from that place or incident. One way they do this is to change formal names, even of those close to them if those people were involved, to pronouns.

For example, if the police were interviewing a suspect in a homicide, they may ask Jim, "Did you kill your best friend, Sam?" In an effort to distance himself from the murder, Jim might say, "No, I did not kill him!"

His best friend was murdered and Jim reduced his friendship to a pronoun.

An indication of a lie.

If you watched the press conference some years back when, then President Clinton, came on television and made the statement, "I did not have sexual relations with ***that woman***, Miss Lewinsky..." He did, finally say her name, but only after he distanced himself by calling her "that woman."

Vocal Tone

Liars get nervous. Because they get nervous the body reacts to that anxiety as we discussed in Flight or Fight and the muscles will tense. The vocal chords are muscles and, like the rest of the muscles in the body, will become tense and the result will be similar to a guitar string that is tightened, the pitch will be higher! It may be a slight increase, but it is usually there.

Rate of Speech

When a person gets nervous they tend to talk

faster. Now, they probably won't talk as fast as those disclaimers at the end of radio commercials for car dealerships, but be cognizant for increases in the rate of speech. This also goes hand-in-hand with the vocal tone. Listen carefully for faster speaking and a higher vocal tone.

Repeat the Question

In order to stall, perhaps the subject thinks a national crisis or a renegade asteroid will interrupt the questioning, the subject may repeat the question you asked back to you.

The repeat of the question does not have to be verbatim, but can be the crux of the question.

QUESTION:

"Dorothy, did you take the money from the counter?"

REPEAT:

"The money on the counter, you're asking me if I took it? No, I did not take it."

Tense Swapping

Under normal circumstances, this is difficult for us to do, even on purpose, but when someone is busy trying to keep their story straight, it can happen without them knowing.

QUESTION:

"Where did you go last night?"

ANSWER:

"Me? Oh, I went with the guys over to Ben's and then I'm going to get your package."

Notice the tense swap?

"I went," past tense and then, "I'm going," future tense."

This is probably a good time for you and me to go over what is called Cognitive Overload.

When someone is attempting to keep their story straight - the lies - the brain is working overtime! But that's just part of it, the subject is not only attempting to keep their story straight, they are trying to keep the truth from accidentally slipping out. The brain is so busy with these processes, it can hardly keep up with everything and mistakes happen.

Allusion / Failure to Deny

Sometimes a liar will not categorically deny they are guilty of anything, but instead they will hedge, beat-around-the-bush, so to speak.

They won't admit nor deny, but they will allude to their innocence. Take for example...

QUESTION:

"Mary, did you take that purse from the break room?"

ANSWER:

"Take the purse? Oh my gosh, no, I've never taken anything that didn't belong to me in my life."

Notice there is no denial, just the allusion that, because she has never taken anything before, she wouldn't now.

She alludes her innocence.

Elusion

Often, a liar trying to divert the conversation will try to change that conversation. One of those ways is to do so mid-sentence. The liar hopes the subject change will stick and the

questioning w

QUESTION:

    "Robir

ANSWER:

    "Me?

your shirt,

Qualifyir

The liar r

try to win you to his side

you are believing their story.

    To do this, you may hear such statements
as:

    "You're with me on this, right?"

    "You understand, don't you?"

    "Can you relate?"

Aggression Toward Questioner or Third Party

The liar may try to deflect the questioning by becoming agitated or angry at being asked about an incident. This is to try to get you to stop questioning them.

you, the person

ay be directed to a

ney can try to pass blame.

ay be real or it may be fake.

wever, if you notice any signs of

is best to back away from the

ng. [We will discuss contempt

uy.]

Statements of agitation or aggression can look like this:

TOWARD THE QUESTIONER
QUESTION:

"Cindy, why did you not turn that marketing report into human resources?"
ANSWER:

"Why is this so important?!!! Is this ALL YOU HAVE TO DO? I cannot believe I am being subjected to this!"

TOWARD A THIRD PARTY

"Danny, human resources old me you were late again for work."

"HUMAN RESOURCES?! What's THEIR problem?? Why don't they just worry about getting us enough help?!!"

Perception Qualifiers

In an effort to distance themselves from the situation, they will often use distancing language.

Without actually admitting anything, they may use phrases such as "As far as I know," "Best I can remember," "As far as I can tell."

QUESTION:

"You were there with Cindy, what did she do with the gun?"

ANSWER:

"As far as I remember, she left it in the box."

"As far as I remember" is different from "She left it in the box" or "I do not know."

Invoking God or Religion

Liars have to try to make you believe their

story and one of the ways that they may use is to invoke God or religion into their statement to you. Somehow, they think that by doing so, you may perhaps roll over and "play dead," immediately believing their story. They probably believe it makes them look more credible.

QUESTION:

"Mindy, did you take the money from the cash drawer?"

ANSWER:

"Me? Oh my goodness, with God as my witness, I never took that money!"

QUESTION:

"Karl, did you lie to Betty about the report?"

ANSWER:

"Oh no, my religion would never allow me to lie."

Conveying vs Convincing

Conveying is simply providing information,

typically truthful information. Convincing is supplying information but doing so in a manner to sway or convince the person of what is being said. One of the things the subject may use to try to convince you that what (s)he is saying is the truth, is to provide you with what I call "Big Information." "Big Information" is nothing more than providing much more information than one would normally expect. This additional information is their attempt to try to prove to you that what they are telling you is, indeed, the truth.

Perhaps you ask the question, "What time did you get home last night?" A simple answer, a conveying answer, would be something like "I got home a little after eleven." An answer that one is giving to ry to convince could look, instead, like, "What time did I get home? Wow, no, I got home a little after eleven, but the reason we were late was we went to this new restaurant on 25th Street and you wouldn't believe the menu! They had everything and I, of course, had to try the nachos and, oh, the flavored tea? It was to die for! It was all awesome! We're going to go back next week and eat there again! It's so much better than that place on 84th Street!"

If you get something like that for an answer to a simple question, be wary of a lie!

Inappropriate Level of Concern

"My God, I can't believe someone actually took the quarter from Ben's desk, how awful! Who would do such a thing? That is so childish and immature, We must find that person and bring them to justice! This is crazy!"

Someone just became overly concerned about a quarter! If you experience such over concern to what is normally a minor event, become suspect.

That works the other way as well.

QUESTION:

"Bill, your best friend was just murdered and I felt I needed to be the one to tell you."

ANSWER:

"Really? Ok."

Someone who seemingly brushes off a major event or situation, be equally concerned and suspect of their involvement.

Verbal / Physical Disconnect

This is another impact of Cognitive Overload. Because the body is so wrapped up in keeping the lies and the fabricated story straight and the truth from coming out, it can make mistakes. These mistakes are what we are looking for.

One of he more common verbal/physical disconnects is the person answering "Yes" or "No" while shaking or nodding their head in the opposite.

For instance, someone verbally answering a question "No," but nodding their head in the affirmative! They may also do the opposite and answer "Yes," but shaking their head no.

Try to do this, it's very hard to do, intentionally!

Behavioral Pause

We don't all have photographic memory and there are times when someone may take a moment to think about something you may have asked them. For instance if you were to ask someone, "What were you doing on January 23rd in 2006, unless that date is important to them due to a birthday, anniversary, or other important event, most people would have to think about what they were doing. That is understandable.

However, if you were to ask the subject a question like, "Did you rob the West Alameda First Commerce Bank on January 23rd in 2006?" and the subject has to think about *that* answer, you may have a problem!!

Of course, if you ask someone what they did for lunch yesterday, a long pause may be suspicious and indicate that they are attempting to come up with an answer that is not the truth.

When asking questions, be cognizant of *what* you ask.

Repeat Same Words Or Phrases Over and Over

Listen for the subject to repeat words or phrases repeatedly. You know what I mean? This is another indicator of lying where having a good baseline helps. You know what I mean? Most of us have known someone who, sometimes quite annoyingly, uses the same word or phrases over and over. You know what I mean?

Okay, be sure to listen for these words or phrases, okay? The repeated use of words or phrases could indicate you are being lied to, okay? Know what I mean?

Over Focus on Insignificant Details

Someone who is lying to you may be evasive on the important facts of the incident, but spend an inordinate amount of time or focus on non-important and insignificant details.

QUESTION:

"David, did you see Jim steal the money from the office?"

ANSWER:

"The money? One time he left work with a pen that belonged to the company, but he brought it back. He just forgot it was in his pocket."

CHAPTER SIX
Physical Indicators

When lying, the individual may show physical movement, or even non movement, that may indicate a lie.

Blading

Someone who is lying to you may blade themselves to your position. In other words, they may turn slightly to their right or left, canting themselves. This is done to limit their exposure to you in the hope that they will not be discovered in their lie. This can happen standing as well as sitting. When sitting, the individual my reposition themselves in their seat or, if in a chair, they may slide the chair to the right or left.

Object Between

As a kid, did you ever hide behind a wall hoping

that no one would see you? Someone who is lying may hold an object in their hand so that, between the two of you, he can *hide* behind it. This is a barrier similar to when you were a kid and would hide and you hoped no one would see you. The liar hopes that the object will somehow shelter them from your perception of their lie.

This object can be most anything including drinking glasses, ink pens, books, purses, anything they can hold and put between you and them.

Looking Down After Answering "No"

"Did you get into the cookie jar?" the mother asks the three year old boy? "No, mommy, not me," as the child looks down at his feet.

Saying "No" to a question and then looking down is an indicator of lying, just as the little boy knew he had been caught, but still denied rummaging in the cookie jar.

Saying "No" and then looking down is due to the person that is lying feeling guilty for having actually told the lie, they do not want to look you eye to eye.

Fake Smile

"A smile covers a multitude of sins" is an oft heard quote and, unless you are privy to what to look for, may do just that!

A fake smile is different from a genuine smile in one respect. Let's discuss.

GENUINE SMILE (DUCHENNE SMILE)

Someone who has a genuine smile will smile with their entire face and that includes their mouth, cheeks, and eyes.

When we smile genuinely there are several muscle pairs that are used and these are:

Muscles Around the Mouth and Cheek

1. Zygomaticus Major
2. Zygomaticus Minor
3. Levator Labii Superioris
4. Risorius
5. Orbicularis Oris

6.   Obicularis Oculi

FAKE SMILE

A fake smile is a forced smile and will usually only include the muscles around the mouth and cheek. There will be no, or extremely little eye movement. Any eye movement will be because of extraneous movement of the cheeks.

Eye Shift

It has been said that the eyes are the window to the soul. Not sure about the soul part, but the eyes are a window to detecting lies!

The first step in using eye shift as an indicator of lying is to determine whether the individual is right or left handed and this can be accomplished several different ways, all of which I have used at one time or another.

• Get the person a bottle of water before you begin questioning. When you give the water to the person, approach them face-to-face straight on as you were going to shake hands.

As you get close, hand them the bottle of water centered between you both and not more to either the right or left side – center! You want them to use their dominant hand so be sure not to force their use of a hand because you put the bottle closer or easier to reach by that hand. It must be receivable equally by either hand.

• Another trick I have used is to drop something in front of them and see which hand they use to pick up the object. I don't like this method as much as you cannot be certain that the object you drop will fall center to them.

• Have the person fill out a form of some type or write something on paper.

• Ask them. This, however, may cause suspicion as to why you are asking.

Rubbing/Scratching Nose or Ear
The fight-or-flight condition goes into play here. Because of this, the person may experience itching or coolness to the nose and/or ears and they may have the need to scratch or warm them.

Feet and Eye Pointing

If someone is lying to you, you may notice the subject keep looking toward a door and/or you may notice the subject's feet pointing toward a door.

The liar probably does not realize this is happening, but is a cue to you that the subject wants to leave the room and the questioning.

This can happen whether the subject is standing or sitting.

Anchor Point Shift

An anchor point is a point or points where the weight of the individual rests. For instance, if the individual is standing with weight equally distributed on both feet, their anchor points are both feet.

If, however, the subject to whom you are talking, is sitting squared in the chair, their anchor points are both buttocks.

If you observe the subject frequently shifting the anchor point, perhaps from right foot to left foot and back again, or from buttock to buttock, you may be experiencing a lie.

Take caution to note that no one is a robot and standing or sitting for extended periods of time can be uncomfortable or exhausting for most anyone. Normal shifting of an anchor point can be normal if the subject is standing or sitting for an extended period of time.

Grooming

Someone who is being deceptive with you may groom themselves. This may be brushing lint, real or imaginary, off heir clothing, adjusting a coat sleeve, painting fingernails, combing hair, putting on lipstick, retying a shoe lace, or any similar action.

Holding or Touching Forehead (Looking Down)

If you observe someone answer "No" holding their head/forehead and then look down, be suspicious that you were just told a lie.

Covering Mouth

Many times, someone telling a lie will cover their mouth. Like a child hiding and not wanting to be discovered, the liar will cover the mouth to, not be discovered. Perhaps by covering their mouth, the lie will not be discovered!

Coughing or Clearing Throat

Because of flight-or-fight, the mouth will become dry. If you observe the individual frequently coughing or clearing he throat, become suspect that you may be being lied to.

Dilated Pupils

Dilation of the pupils of the eyes is a response to the body's actions in fight-or-flight as we previously discussed.

Pupils change size according to the amount of light the eyes are expose to, but they also respond to the autonomic nervous system composed of two branches, the sympathetic and parasympathetic nervous system.

The parasympathetic nervous system is responsible for resting the eyes and is what causes the pupils to constrict and the sympathetic nervous system is responsible for he eyes dilating relating to stress – the fight-or-flight response.

Further, the muscles in the iris respond according to the signals. The sphincter muscles are similar to concentric rings that can constrict as much as two millimeters in diameter. The dilator muscles organized like spokes on a bicycle, can cause the pupil to open, dilate, as much as eight millimeters in diameter.

As you are observing your subject and see the pupils dilate, you have probably just been told a lie, well, unless the lights just dimmed!

Also, be sure they just have not just come from an eye exam!

Blinking

Detecting lies can be a daunting task, you have to watch everything! Well, let's add the eyelids to the list! I know, right? Well, you're already watching their eyes for eye shift and dilated pupils, so, while you're there, keep a watch on that blinking!

When talking with someone and they have lied to you, you may notice their blinking increase as much as 800 percent!

The average number of blinks per minute vary, but most people blink an average of 15 times per minute – every four seconds. Now, of course, this can vary. Someone may blink more or less, this is just an average. This is where having a baseline comes in handy!

When watching for blinking variation, you want to watch for their blinking **after** they answer. During the answer, they will blink the normal rate or maybe ever so slightly slower, but after the answer, if it is a lie, they may blink 8 times faster!

[NOTE: A blink lasts approximately $1/10^{th}$ of a second and, on average, we blink about 21,600 times per day. You don't particularly need to know that for our purposes here, but I thought I'd share that with you!

Hey, you never know when you may be a contestant on Jeopardy®!

> "I'll take Eyes for $500 Alex."
>
> "21,600 times a day."
>
> "What would the blinking rate of the average person per day, Alex!"]
>
> You're welcome!

Suprasternal Notch

Animals in the wild will typically attack their opponent at their neck. Someone who is lying may very well reach at the area of their suprasternal notch when lying.

Where is the suprasternal notch? Place your finger on your sternum (the area on the front of your chest where the rib bones connect) and follow your sternum upward until you feel the sternum end. A that point you will feel a notch. That notch is your suprasternal notch – the top of the ribs and the base of your neck.

If someone is lying, you may notice them reach up to the area of their suprasternal notch. Men will often do this by way of adjusting their necktie and women, by fidgeting with a necklace. However, this may also take place without either and just simply the liar touching the suprasternal notch area with their fingers.

Lowering or Hiding Thumbs

The thumbs are points of dominance and when shown, typically represent a feel of confidence by the person. If you observe the thumbs lower or covered by the palms, you may be being lied to.

Finger Tenting

When someone tents their fingers, they typically have a level of confidence about themselves and this confidence of self-assuredness can be visualized, at times, by their tenting of their fingers.

Tenting is the position of the fingertips (usually including the thumbs as well) of the right and left hands pressed against each other bu the palms are distanced at the bottom causing a *tenting* of the hands.

You may notice, when a person has his fingers tented and begins to lie, that, not only does the tent go away, but he also covers his thumbs at the same time.

Lip Compression / Lip Biting

Someone who is lying to you may compress or bite their lips. This is typically due to anxiety and nervousness.

Answer Ventilation

If someone is about to lie to you after you ask them a question, watch for answer ventilation. This usually in a pronounced inhale and exhale prior to that person answering your question.

Leaning Back (Distancing)

If you are in a conversation with someone and they lean back in their chair, be aware that they may be lying.

Leaning back is a way for them to try to distance themselves from you.

Sweating

As soon as the human body begins to be stressed, it begins to sweat.

This is, as you will remember, part of the flight-or-fight activity by the body.

The sweat produced due to stress comes from the apocrine glands, where sweat due to body temperature increases and exercise, comes from the eccrine glands.

Depending on the situation, you will probably notice sweat first on the forehead or upper lip of the subject.

Sweating does not necessarily indicate lying, but is still significant as it does indicate stress of the individual due to the situation or questions.

NOTE: You will want to make sure that the subject did not just complete a meal with jalapenos or habaneros or consume a large amount of alcohol, both of which may cause sweating.

Licking Lips

This is the result of the flight-or-fight stage. As we have previously referenced, when lying, the mouth becomes dry and the liar may lick their lips as they will be also be dry.

Hiding Eyes

Have you ever tried to avoid someone because you were embarrassed about something? The same principle applies here. A liar, being subconsciously embarrassed that she is lying to you, may cover her eyes at the point of the lie.

A NOTE ABOUT
SIGNS OF CONTEMPT

Be cognizant of those who may become frustrated or angry with you in a conversation. Be even more aware of anyone who shows signs of contempt toward you.

<u>Contempt is one of the more dangerous of emotions</u> as it can be a lasting and strong emotion and it, basically, is the repulsive feeling of one toward another.

Be particular observant for any signs of

• The upper lip of the subject raised up on one side, even if slightly.

• A sarcastic verbal overtone.

• Someone rolls their eyes.

Often, the signs of contempt can be expressed as microexpressions and take place quickly. Be very observant.

If you find someone expressing contempt during your conversation, I would advise leaving the conversation and distancing yourself from that individual.

ABOUT THE AUTHOR

Steven spent twenty-one years in a career as police officer and SVU detective. Steven was the arresting officer of The Clairemont Killer (serial killer) featured on America's Most Wanted® and case coverage on such television networks as Investigation Discovery™, The Discovery Channel™, FOX™, and TruTV™ as well as the New York Times™ and Los Angeles Times™.

Steven developed, implemented, and supervised a new Special Victim's Unit (SVU) criminal investigative sex crimes against children division. He was the arresting officer of a Fugitive from Justice on Canada's Most Wanted and worked closely with the FBI, DOJ United States Attorney's Office, United States Postal Inspector's Service, and Alabama Attorney General's office under Troy King (2006-2011).

He received two awards for Police Officer of the Year as well as numerous departmental and civilian commendations.

Steven now uses his experience as a speaker and trainer presenting *How to Catch a Liar* seminars across the country to police academies, colleges and universities, corporations, businesses, organizations, and associations. Steven is also an author penning true crime books (all of Steven's books have five star ratings).

Steven is a regular guest on *Crime Stories with Nancy Grace* and is a contributor to various magazines including *Law Enforcement Today*.

As a radio show host, he can be heard each week as host of the acclaimed Crime & Forensics aired on KCAA in Los Angeles and on great radio stations across the country. Crime & Forensics can also be heard on Spotify™, iTunes™, iHeart Radio™, Stitcher™, Spreaker™, and other media sources. He is also frequently a co-host of House of Mystery

Radio Show on KKNW in Seattle, the number one crime and history radio show in the United States.

You may reach the author through his website www.StevenDavidLampley.com

HOW TO
CATCH
a LIAR

Book Steven to present

How to Catch a Liar

to your corporation, college, university,
police academy, or organization!

You can also partner with Steven to
present a ticketed event
for the public in your city!

www.StevenDavidLampley.com

POLICE

The Real Story Behind the Scenes

One Officer's Story.

Former Twenty-One Year Career Police Officer and
Undercover Sex Crimes SVU Detective

STEVEN DAVID
LAMPLEY

Coming Soon!

A behind the scenes look into the very real life of a police
officer. *Police: The Real Story Behind the Scenes* takes you into
the street, in the patrol car, and into his home.
A very revealing book. It's all laid right out on the table!
You will laugh and cry, but you won't forget this book!

36737436R00058

Made in the USA
San Bernardino, CA
24 May 2019